NEW VANGUARD 280

WORLD WAR II GERMAN SUPER-HEAVY SIEGE GUNS

**MARC ROMANYCH
AND MARTIN RUPP**

ILLUSTRATED BY ADAM TOOBY AND
ANDREA RICCIARDI DI GAUDESI

OSPREY PUBLISHING

Bloomsbury Publishing Plc

PO Box 883, Oxford, OX1 9PL, UK

1385 Broadway, 5th Floor, New York, NY 10018, USA

E-mail: info@ospreypublishing.com

www.ospreypublishing.com

OSPREY is a trademark of Osprey Publishing Ltd

First published in Great Britain in 2020

A catalogue record for this book is available from the British Library.

ISBN: PB 9781472837172; eBook 9781472837189;
ePDF 9781472837165; XML 9781472837158

20 21 22 23 24   10 9 8 7 6 5 4 3 2 1

Index by Rob Munro
Typeset by PDQ Digital Media Solutions, Bungay, UK
Printed and bound by Bell & Bain Ltd., Glasgow G46 7UQ

Osprey Publishing supports the Woodland Trust, the UK's leading woodland conservation charity.

To find out more about our authors and books visit
www.ospreypublishing.com. Here you will find extracts, author interviews, details of forthcoming events and the option to sign up for our newsletter.

Authors' Acknowledgements

The authors wish to thank Greg Heuer for his extensive help with reference material and photographs, and 3D computer models that served as the basis for this book's art illustrations. We also wish to thank our wives for their encouragement and support as we researched and wrote this book.

CONTENTS

WORLD WAR II GERMAN SUPER-HEAVY SIEGE GUNS

INTRODUCTION

As the Third Reich prepared for war, it faced the same problem that had confronted its predecessor, Imperial Germany, nearly 20 years earlier on the eve of World War I. Germany was encircled by strong fortifications and needed artillery to destroy them. However, unlike 1914, when the Imperial German Army had an arsenal of large-calibre siege guns, in the mid-1930s, the Third Reich had none. As it rearmed, the army ordered artillery manufacturers Krupp and Rheinmetall-Borsig to build super-heavy siege guns capable of destroying France's Maginot Line, the strongest fortification in Europe. These new super-heavy artillery pieces were much larger and more powerful than their World War I counterparts, but were also far more difficult to manufacture and, as war drew near, not one of the guns had been completed. As a stop-gap, the army equipped itself with World War I-vintage siege guns, primarily Skoda-made artillery taken from Czechoslovakia in 1938–39, and then went to war.

During World War II, the German Army employed siege guns during campaigns in Poland, Belgium, France and the Soviet Union. At its zenith, during the siege of Sevastopol in the Crimea in 1942, Germany's siege artillery totalled 30 guns, including the massive self-propelled 60cm Karl mortars and the 80cm Dora railway gun. By 1943, as Germany was forced onto the defensive, the need for siege artillery rapidly diminished and the guns were either retired from service or employed as heavy artillery in support of the armies on the Eastern and Western Fronts.

THE RETURN OF FORTRESS EUROPE

Before World War I, the European armies emphasized permanent fortifications to defend their borders and cities. However, the success of German 42cm and Austrian 30.5cm

Germany manufactured several super-heavy siege guns for the specific purpose of destroying modern reinforced concrete fortifications such as France's Maginot Line. Seen here is the first prototype self-propelled 60cm Karl-Gerät mortar. (M. Romanych)

siege guns against Belgian, French and Russian forts in the first two years of the Great War rendered large permanent fortifications obsolete, and armies on both sides abandoned such fortifications for trench systems reinforced with small concrete casemates and shelters. By the end of the war, both permanent fortifications and siege artillery were out of favour with the warring armies.

After the war, Germany's siege guns were either confiscated by the Allies or destroyed in accordance with the armistice and Versailles Treaty. Only one siege gun survived, a 42cm Gamma howitzer that was dismantled and hidden by Krupp. Similarly, most siege artillery of Germany's wartime ally, Austro-Hungary, was seized by Yugoslavia, Hungary, Czechoslovakia, Italy and Romania.

The Versailles Treaty not only destroyed Germany's siege artillery, but also sought to prevent the design and manufacture of new pieces. To circumvent the treaty's restrictions, the Reichswehr (Germany's armed forces from 1919 until 1935) surreptitiously established manufacturing arrangements between its two artillery manufacturers – Krupp and Rheinmetall – and the firms of Bofors in Sweden and Waffenfabrik Solothurn in Switzerland. However, the design of siege guns was ignored in favour of smaller, more mobile pieces, and the manufacture of new super-heavy guns had to wait until after the Third Reich renounced the Versailles Treaty in 1935 and expanded its military rearmament programme.

Suspicious that Germany was secretly rearming, adjacent countries began to construct permanent fortification systems in the late 1920s. First, France began building the Maginot Line in Alsace and Lorraine, then Belgium rebuilt its defences at Liège and Namur, and the Netherlands constructed a series of blockhouse lines along its border with Germany. Inspired by France's Maginot Line, Czechoslovakia heavily fortified its borders with Germany and Austria, and Poland built fortified positions to defend itself from a German invasion. Even neutral Switzerland erected border defences to deter German aggression. Central Europe was a fortress once again, much as it had been on the eve of World War I, and Germany, now encircled by fortifications, decided to equip its army with siege artillery.

DESIGN AND DEVELOPMENT

Although the German Army did not officially designate any artillery pieces as siege guns, it did build super-heavy artillery pieces for siege operations. For the purposes of this book, German World War II siege guns are defined as super-heavy mortars and howitzers, 28cm or larger in calibre, designed or used to destroy fortified targets. Additionally, German Army designations of artillery pieces as either *Mörser* (mortar) or *Haubitze* (howitzer) should not be taken strictly because the terms overlapped and were different in World Wars I and II.

Before and during World War II, artillery manufacturers Krupp and Rheinmetall built three different types of super-heavy siege guns for the German Army: a 60cm self-propelled mortar, an 80cm super-heavy railway gun and a mobile 35.5cm long-range howitzer. Designing and manufacturing such large and complex artillery pieces was a lengthy process and the military's need for siege artillery grew more immediate as the prospect of war drew nearer. To solve the problem, the Army High Command had Krupp reassemble the vintage 42cm Gamma howitzer hidden at its factory, and then, when the opportunity presented itself in 1938 and 1939, it acquired a large number of World War I-era Skoda siege guns from the Czechoslovakian Army.

SELF-PROPELLED SIEGE GUNS

Development of a self-propelled siege gun began in 1936 after artillery manufacturer Rheinmetall created a concept for a ground-mounted 80cm mortar with a 1,000m range. The proposed weapon lacked mobility and range, so Rheinmetall reworked the concept into a smaller 60cm mortar with a range of 3,000m that could be disassembled into several components transported on wheeled vehicles. However, the mobility of the weapon was still below expectations, so Rheinmetall redesigned the concept again. This design, which eventually became the 60cm 'Gerät 040' or 'Karl-Gerät', evolved several times until approved for production in March 1938.

1. Muzzle-Loading 60cm Mortar (Conceptual Design): Rheinmetall's first design for a self-propelled siege gun featured a muzzle-loading mortar with a hand-operated crane for loading ammunition into the mortar's muzzle. To fire, the mortar's barrel would have to be super-elevated and then flipped over to face in the opposite direction. Key features of this design included an internal dual recoil system and a spade mounted on the rear of the tracked carrier. This design never progressed beyond a concept.

2. Breech-Loading 60cm Mortar (Conceptual Design): Rheinmetall's second design was a breech-loading mortar. It too was mounted on a tracked carrier with a crane to load ammunition, but the gun now faced the direction of fire. The mortar had a more robust recoil mechanism mounted above the barrel, but a spade was still needed to anchor the carrier in place. This design also remained a concept and never left the drawing board.

3. 60cm Karl-Gerät (Production Model): The final design was significantly different from the previous concepts. The mortar faced the rear of the carrier so that the weapon could be driven quickly out of its firing position. The previous designs' recoil spade was replaced by a carriage slide inside the carrier's hull. In all, six Karl mortars were built. Modifications to the vehicle engine, drive train and suspension were continually made during the production cycle of the mortars, so none of the six weapons was identical. Particularly notable was the suspension system. The first two Karl mortars had eight road rubber wheels per side, while later weapons (like that shown in this illustration) had 11 steel road wheels.

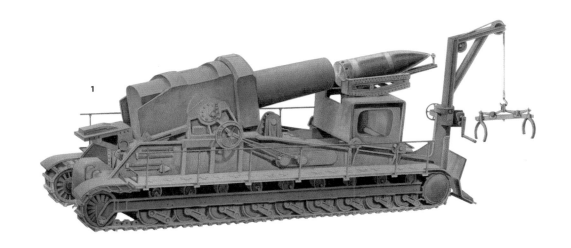

1

2

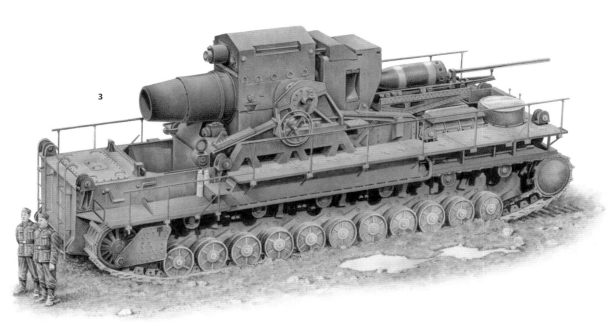

3

60cm and 54cm Karl-Gerät

As the first fortifications of France's Maginot Line neared completion, the German Army began seeking artillery to bombard them. The army, knowing that the Maginot fortifications were built to withstand a direct hit from a 42cm projectile, the largest calibre used by Germany in World War I, queried both Krupp and Rheinmetall about what calibre weapon was needed to destroy the Maginot Line. The enquiry initiated two different super-heavy artillery development programmes.

The first siege gun considered by the German Army was a super-heavy self-propelled mortar. Rheinmetall began working the concept in 1934 and initially proposed an 80cm ground-mounted mortar. However, concerns about the weapon's mobility and range resulted in a series of redesigns until, in March 1938, the army approved Rheinmetall's design for a self-propelled 60cm mortar and ordered seven of the weapons. Although manufacture of the first piece proceeded quickly, it was not ready in time for use against the Maginot Line in May 1940. Yet, even with the capture of the Maginot Line, construction of the 60cm mortar continued, with six guns completed and delivered to the amy from February to July 1941. The seventh piece, which was re-engineered with a smaller 54cm calibre barrel, was not finished until 1944.

Confusingly, the 60cm self-propelled mortar had several names and designations during its life. While in testing, the first weapon was given the cover name 'Gerät 040' and, as each subsequent piece was built, it was numbered in order of production by a roman numeral, I–VII. In 1941, the Gerät 040's official designation was changed to 'Gerät-Karl' and then again in 1942 to 'Karl-Gerät'. After being fielded, artillery units nicknamed the guns: I – Adam; II – Eva; III – Odin; IV – Thor; V – Loki; VI – Ziu; VII (unknown).

The Gerät 040 was a massive weapon, measuring 3m tall, 11m long and 3m wide, and weighing an astounding 123 metric tonnes. Its two primary components were the gun and the tracked carrier. The gun was a conventional, fixed-mount mortar similar in design to a coastal or fortress artillery barbette piece. The gun tube was 60cm (23.8in) calibre and short (about 5m). To absorb the force generated when firing, the Gerät 040 had a dual recoil system. One mechanism was built into the gun cradle to brake the barrel's recoil and return it to firing position, and a second was mounted on

The primary means of transporting the Karl mortar was by rail. Despite its great bulk and size, the railway transporter with mortar could pass over, and through, existing bridges and tunnels. (M. Romanych)

the bottom of the gun carriage to allow the gun to slide backwards inside the carrier's hull. To relieve pressure on the suspension and increase stability, the hull was lowered onto the ground when firing. The mortar was fired at elevations between 55 and 70 degrees and had limited traverse – four degrees – which was enough to adjust fire on a specific target. For larger changes in direction of fire, the tracked carrier was shifted by turning it on its tracks. To facilitate loading of the rounds and propellant, a loading tray with a hand-cranked rammer was attached to the gun carriage.

The carrier was a large steel box hull partitioned into three sections. The front section contained the engine, power train and compartments for the driver and assistant driver. The first four Gerät 040s were built with 580hp gasoline engines, but because of reliability problems, an 800hp diesel was used in subsequent vehicles and eventually replaced by gasoline engines. Depending on the type of engine, the Gerät 040's top speed was 10km/h. The centre section was a large open compartment for the gun. The rear section contained the batteries for the engine and the gear system for lowering the carrier to the ground. The bottom of the carrier had a grid of steel grips that held the carrier in place when firing.

The Gerät 040 was designed to be self-propelled for only a few kilometres, typically from its assembly area to the firing position. For long-distance travel, the weapon was moved by rail via specially built rail transporter that, when loaded with the oversized Gerät 040, could fit through existing bridges and tunnels. For shorter distances, the Gerät 040 was disassembled and loaded onto trailers towed by artillery tractors.

Two types of projectiles were made for the Gerät 040. The first projectile was a *schwere Betongranate* (heavy anti-concrete projectile). The projectile was 2.5m long and weighed 2,170kg. The Gerät 040's maximum range when firing the heavy projectile was 4,300m. The projectile could penetrate up to 2.5m of reinforced concrete. In 1942, to extend the range of the Gerät 040, a 1,700kg *leichte Betongranate* (light anti-concrete projectile) was developed. The lighter projectile could be fired to 6,640m. Firing tables estimated that only 50 per cent of rounds were likely to strike within a 19m x 3m target area, which was surprising low, considering that the mortar was designed to fire only a few rounds on its target. To facilitate firing operations, a tracked ammunition carrier was built for the Gerät 040 by modifying a Mark IV tank chassis. The carrier could hold four projectiles with propellant charges and cartridge cases. An electric-driven crane was mounted on the carrier's hull for transferring the projectiles, propellant and cartridge cases to the Gerät 040.

The Gerät 040 had a crew of 21 soldiers. After offloading from its rail transporter or road trailers, the Gerät 040 was assembled and driven under its own power to its firing position. An ideal position was located behind a hill or woods, to avoid enemy observation. Before the Gerät 040 arrived, the firing position was cleared of brush and other material and, if necessary, the ground levelled. Upon arrival at the firing site, the Gerät 040 was backed into position with its gun facing the in the general direction of the target and then laid into its azimuth of fire. The carrier was then lowered to the ground, the gun carriage unlocked and crew platforms were put in place. A projectile and cartridge case were transferred from the ammunition carrier to the mortar's loading tray and pushed into the breech using hand-cranked rammer. The barrel was then set to proper azimuth and elevation. Before firing, the gun crew and ammunition carrier moved away from the weapon. The process was repeated until all allocated rounds were fired or the Gerät 040 had to move. A crew of a Gerät 040 could thus achieve a rate of fire of one round every ten minutes.

The Gerät 040's short range was a concern throughout its development and operational life, and in 1941 Rheinmetall was ordered to design a smaller-calibre (54cm) and longer-barrelled gun for the Gerät 040 with a range of 10,000m. The new weapon – designated the Gerät 041 – was completed in the summer of 1944. Six additional barrels were manufactured to eventually replace worn-out 60cm barrels on the Gerät 040s. To convert a Gerät 040 to a 041 required a few minor changes to the gun cradle, but

B   MOVING THE 60CM KARL MORTAR

The Karl mortar was designed to self-propel over short distances. For long distance travel, it was transported by rail using specially built railway wagons. A pair of massive five-axle wagons with large pedestal-mounted trusses were used to lift and suspend the entire gun and carrier between the two wagons. The trusses were attached to lift points on the carrier, and four powerful hydraulic jacks raised the trusses and mortar into the suspended travel position, creating a single unit for transport. When the railway wagons were moved without the mortar, the trusses were coupled together, and the wagons were connected with tow bars. The rest of the unit's equipment was transported on standard railway wagons.

For road travel, the Karl mortar was disassembled using a 35-tonne crane and loaded onto special heavy-duty trailers. The gun was removed from the carrier, broken down into three pieces and placed on three 16-wheel trailers – one for the barrel and breech block, one for the cradle and carriage (with lower recoil mechanism) and one for the upper recoil mechanism and loading tray. The tracked carrier was driven under its own power onto a 24-wheel trailer. Half-tracked artillery tractors were used to tow the trailers. To cross bridges, the tracked carrier had to be removed from its trailer, driven separately across the bridge and reloaded onto the trailer for further transport.

Getting a Karl mortar into action at the front was an arduous task. It was transported by rail to a rail head, off-loaded, disassembled and then loaded onto road trailers. Artillery tractors towed the loaded trailers to a location near the firing sites, where the mortars were re-assembled and then driven under their own power into firing position. The process was repeated in reverse order to withdraw the Karl mortars from action. A collapsible gantry crane accompanied the mortars wherever they went.

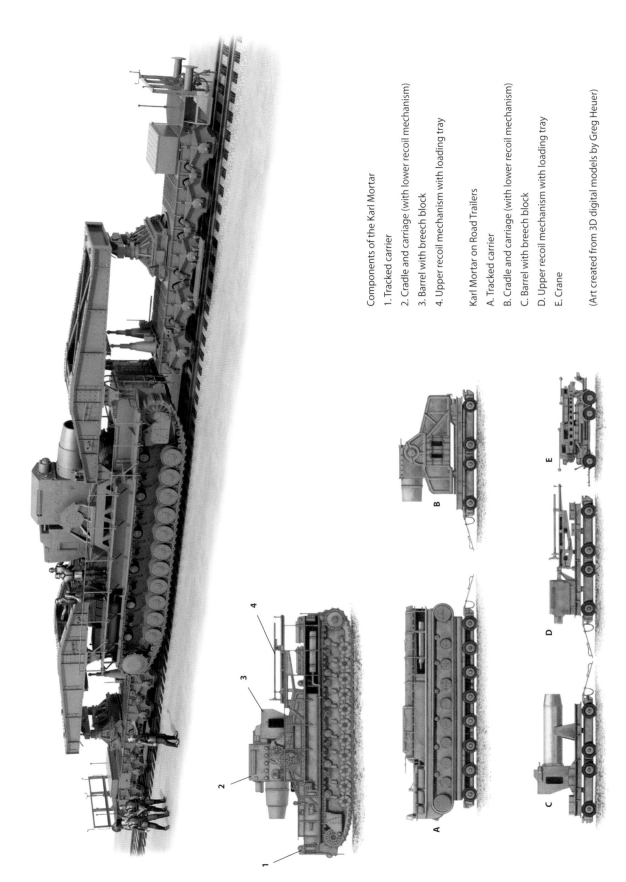

Components of the Karl Mortar

1. Tracked carrier

2. Cradle and carriage (with lower recoil mechanism)

3. Barrel with breech block

4. Upper recoil mechanism with loading tray

Karl Mortar on Road Trailers

A. Tracked carrier

B. Cradle and carriage (with lower recoil mechanism)

C. Barrel with breech block

D. Upper recoil mechanism with loading tray

E. Crane

(Art created from 3D digital models by Greg Heuer)

otherwise the carriage and tracked vehicle remained the same. The 54cm projectile was a 1,250kg 'light' round that could penetrate up to 3.5m of concrete. Operation, rate of fire and accuracy of the Gerät 041 were the same as the Gerät 040.

80cm Railway Gun Gustav-Gerät

As Rheinmetall was working on the 60cm Gerät 040, Krupp began developing an even larger artillery piece: an 80cm (31½in) railway gun which, when completed, was the largest artillery piece ever built and used in combat. Unlike the short-range Gerät 040 that had to get close to its target, the 80cm railway gun was designed to shell fortifications up to 48km away. The genesis of the super-gun was in 1934 when the Army High Command asked Krupp, which was already designing several models of large-calibre railway guns, about the feasibility of building an artillery piece to bombard the Maginot Line. Krupp's gun design bureau, headed by chief engineer Erich 'Kanonen' Müller, calculated ballistic data for 70cm, 80cm, 85cm and 100cm artillery pieces; however, no further design work was performed. The idea was rekindled in 1936 when Adolf Hitler visited the Krupp works and asked Müller about the possibility of building a super-gun capable of penetrating even the strongest fortifications of the Maginot Line. Müller calculated that a 7-tonne projectile fired at high angle could penetrate up to 8m of reinforced concrete and that such a projectile would require an artillery piece weighing at least 1,000 metric tonnes. Müller's project team created several designs for such a gun, including a self-propelled tracked version, before finally settling on an 80cm rail-mounted gun. A set of drawings was produced, and in early 1937 the army approved the design and ordered three of the guns, with the first to be delivered by early 1940, the second in 1941 and the third in 1944.

Named the 'Gustav-Gerät' by Krupp, the gun was a conventional design built to enormous proportions. Construction began in late 1937, but a timeline to build the gun in three years was optimistic. Not only did the size and weight of the gun present Krupp with innumerable manufacturing challenges, but Krupp also had to build workshops and fabricate equipment for manufacturing the gun's components. Technical problems with forging the barrel and breech assembly delayed manufacture of the gun so much that it was not completed in early 1940 in time for the attack on the Maginot Line. Yet construction of the Gustav-Gerät continued, possibly because Hitler thought the gun could be used for an attack on Gibraltar. The barrel was finally finished in late 1940, mounted to a test stand at the Hillersleben artillery range and proof-fired in August and September 1941. Four shots were fired against a 3.5m-thick reinforced concrete wall, a 60cm metal plate and an 80cm metal plate, and all three targets were easily penetrated. By the year's end, the Gustav-Gerät was assembled at the Rügenwalde proving ground and fired eight times to function-test the weapon and create firing tables. In early 1942, the weapon underwent acceptance testing. Five years after construction began and two years later than estimated, the gun was ready for the army and officially designated the 80cm Kanone (*Eisenbahnlafette*) (80cm Cannon, Railway Carriage), abbreviated as 80cm K(E).

The gun's crew nicknamed it 'Dora', and after that 'Dora-Gerät' or Dora were widely used as the official references to the gun.

Construction of the first 80cm K(E) Gustav-Gerät railway gun began in 1937. Four years later, in 1941, the gun was assembled and test-fired at the Rügenwalde proving ground. The gun was later officially named 'Dora-Gerät', or simply 'Dora' after a nickname given by its crew. The second gun, 'schwerer Gustav', or just 'Gustav', was completed in 1943. (G. Heuer)

Krupp then manufactured a second gun, named 'schwerer Gustav 2' (Heavy Gustav 2), which was identical to Dora except for the barrel lining and coupling mechanism that joined the barrel's two sections. 'Schwerer Gustav', or just 'Gustav', was test fired at Hillersleben in early August 1942 and acceptance tested at Rügenwalde in February 1943. The third gun, named 'Langer Gustav' (Long Gustav), was never completed. Before building the gun, Krupp proposed increasing its range to 110km by reducing the barrel's calibre to 52cm and extending its length from 32m to 48m. The army approved the design in May 1943, but the project ended when Allied bombing heavily damaged Krupp's factory at Essen in 1944.

The Gustav-Gerät was 47m long, 7m wide and 11.5m high, and weighed an astounding 1,350 metric tonnes. Its two main components were the gun assembly and the railway carriage. The gun assembly had seven major sub-components: barrel, barrel jacket, cradle assembly, breechblock, trunnion assembly, gun platform and loading platform. The barrel was 32.5m long and consisted of two sections coupled together and inserted into a barrel jacket that mated it to the cradle assembly. Attached to the rear of the barrel was the breechblock. Together, the barrel and breech block weighed 400 metric tonnes. The cradle assembly contained a recoil and recuperator system of four large cylinders that braked the barrel's recoil and returned it to firing position. The cradle assembly was attached to the trunnion assembly, which in turn was mounted to the gun platform. Inside the gun platform was the mechanism that raised and lowered the barrel. Attached to the gun platform was a loading platform with two ammunition lifts (one for the projectiles and one for the propellant) and a hydraulic mechanism for delivering ammunition to the breech. On the bottom side of the loading platform was a power plant that provided the electricity for the various motors needed to operate the gun.

The railway carriage consisted of three major sub-components: upper carriage, lower carriage and bogie units. The railway carriage was like other railway gun carriages, except that it was four to five times larger and operated on two sets of parallel railway tracks. The carriage was mounted on four bogie units. Each bogie unit was comprised of two five-axle bogies joined

C ASSEMBLING THE SUPER-HEAVY DORA RAILWAY GUN

Assembling Dora was an engineering feat requiring a closely choreographed shunting of loaded railway wagons to and from the assembly site. Piece-by-piece, the gun's components were brought to the site, offloaded and mounted with the aid of two 10-tonne gantry cranes (the 10-tonnes refers to the weight of the cranes, not their lifting capacity). The first step in the process was to assemble and move the bogie units into place. Next, the left and right halves of the upper and lower carriages were off-loaded, placed on the bogie units and bolted together. With assembly of the railway carriage complete, work began on putting the gun assembly together. The gun platform was lifted onto the carriage, followed by the trunnion and cradle assemblies, and then the loading platform with its power generation unit and ammunition lifts. The last step was to insert the barrel into the cradle and attach the breech block. During assembly, steam locomotives were used to move the railway wagons between the marshalling yard and the assembly site.

Dora was assembled in building block fashion. In this scene, a gantry crane is setting the right side of the trunnion assembly onto the railway carriage. The other half of the trunnion assembly is still loaded on its railway wagon. A steam locomotive is ready to remove the wagon once it is unloaded. The cradle assembly, loaded on its railway wagon, is in position next to the locomotive.

Mounting the barrel was the most challenging part of assembling the gun. As shown in this scene, both gantry cranes, working together, were used to align and insert the rear half of the barrel into the barrel jacket. Once the rear section was seated, it was locked in place and the gantry cranes lifted the front half to insert it into the front end of the barrel jacket.

Two large gantry cranes were needed to assemble the Gustav-Gerät railway guns. Here the left half of the gun platform is being lowered onto the upper carriage during acceptance testing of Dora at Rügenwalde in early 1942. (G. Heuer)

together by a large steel beam and plate bolster. In total, the Gustav-Gerät had 80 wheels. The upper and lower carriages sat on the bogie units. Both carriages were massive steel girder and plate structures that could support the weight of the gun assembly and withstand the massive force generated when the gun fired. The purpose of the upper carriage was to raise the height of the gun assembly, so the barrel had sufficient space to recoil when firing at a high angle. Mounted to the bottom of the lower carriage were a series of floats, that were lowered onto the firing track to stabilize the railway carriage as a firing platform and hold the Gustav-Gerät in place.

In addition to the gun itself, several major pieces of support equipment were built for the Gustav-Gerät. For assembly and disassembly of the gun, there were two massive rail-mounted gantry cranes that could straddle the gun while carrying the heaviest and largest of its components. Four special D311 diesel-electric locomotives were provided for moving the Gustav-Gerät on its firing track. Additionally, six temperature-controlled armoured railway wagons were made for transporting and storing the ammunition.

Because of its size and weight, the Gustav-Gerät could only move by rail. For transport, the gun and its major components were dismantled into pieces that met the size and weight limitations of rail shipment. The barrel was disassembled into two 16m-long sections while the trunnion assembly, gun platform, upper and lower carriages were divided longitudinally into left and right pieces that were no wider than a standard railway wagon. Most of the pieces were transported on custom-built railway wagons. Twenty-five railway wagons were needed to transport the gun's components, and another 18 railway wagons carried the gantry cranes, workshops, ancillary equipment and accessories needed to assemble and operate the gun.

Two types of projectiles were made for the Gustav-Gerät: an anti-concrete projectile and a lighter high-explosive projectile. The anti-concrete projectile was 3.6m in length, weighed 7.1 metric tonnes and had a 250kg explosive charge. The projectile could penetrate 1m of steel, 8m of reinforced concrete or 32m of earth. The range of the Gustav-Gerät was 38km when firing the anti-concrete round. The high-explosive round weighed 4.8 metric tonnes and could be fired 48km. Up to 2,240kg of powder, packed into large cloth bags, were used for the propellant charge. Depending on the type of projectile and the desired range, the gun was fired with either two or three charges. A cartridge case was used to seal the breech behind the bags of propellant.

Several weeks were needed to prepare the Gustav-Gerät's firing position. The site consisted of a rail spur from a main rail line, a marshalling yard where the gun was assembled and a firing track from which the gun shelled its targets. The marshalling yard was a set of three parallel railway tracks flanked by rails for the gantry cranes. Nearby, on the spur line, was a small rail yard for shunting railway cars during assembly of the gun. The firing track, located between the marshalling yard and front line, was comprised of two parallel curved railway tracks along which the Gustav-Gerät was moved to point its barrel in the direction of the target. To withstand the force of Gustav-Gerät's recoil, the firing track was built with closely set railway ties and special metal floats to hold the gun carriage in place when the gun fired.

The Gustav-Gerät had a crew of 500 soldiers. A number of Krupp civilian technicians accompanied the gun to provide specialized knowledge for operating and maintaining it. Firing operations were lengthy and complex. When a target was selected, firing data were calculated to determine the range, azimuth and elevation, and then corrected based on environmental factors such as air temperature and wind direction. The gun was then moved into position by diesel-electric locomotives, and the railway carriage's floats were lowered to hold the gun in place. The ammunition wagons were brought in behind the gun, and a projectile, propellant charges and cartridge case were transferred from the wagons to the gun, sent to the loading platform by lift, transferred to mechanical loading cars and then rammed into the breech with a hydraulic ramming mechanism. After being loaded, the barrel was elevated to the correct angle of fire. Before firing, the ammunition wagons were removed and the crew dismounted the gun. The Gustav-Gerät's maximum rate of fire was three rounds an hour, but that rate could not be

When assembled, the Gustav-Gerät was 47m long, 7m wide, 11.5m high and weighed an astounding 1,350 tonnes. Seen here at Rügenwalde, the gun is awaiting installation of the second section of its barrel. (NARA)

maintained for more than three or four rounds because of the need to spot the impact of each round and constantly adjust the gun's firing data.

35.5cm Haubitze M1

While the Karl and Gustav super-guns were being developed, the army also ordered Rheinmetall to build a smaller-calibre, more mobile heavy artillery piece that could penetrate up to 1m of concrete at a range of 20km. Unlike the super-heavy siege guns, the weapon was not specifically designed to attack the Maginot Line, but was intended to bombard smaller fortifications. Design work was initiated in 1935 and proceeded quickly, with the gun approved for manufacture in 1938. Designated the 35.5cm Haubitze M1, the weapon was a modern design that borrowed several features – notably, a dual recoil system and ground platform – used by Rheinmetall's other long-range heavy artillery pieces. The army ordered nine M1 howitzers, of which eight were built. The first piece was delivered in December 1939, in time for the invasion of France, but then production was halted for two-and-a-half years until mid-1942 when five more howitzers were built. A seventh piece was manufactured a year later in May 1943 and the eighth, and last, howitzer was completed in March 1944.

The M1 was a *Bettungsgeschütz* (foundation gun), meaning that its carriage was mounted on a ground platform. The weapon consisted of two primary components – the howitzer and the ground platform – which together weighed 78 metric tonnes. The howitzer had a 10m-long barrel and a two-piece carriage. The top part of the carriage held the barrel and cradle, four hydro-pneumatic recoil cylinders, the elevation mechanism for the barrel and other components needed to operate the gun such as the crew platform, loading wagon and ammunition winch. The top carriage was mated to a lower, or bottom, carriage which raised the overall height of the howitzer so the barrel could elevate and fire at a high angle (up to 75 degrees). The bottom carriage rested on a two-piece ground platform. The front part of the platform was a large square steel beam-and-plate structure anchored to the ground by ten long metal spades, and had a built-in turntable for all-around traverse and a recoil mechanism that worked in conjunction with the gun's recoil cylinders. The rear platform was smaller than the front platform and was not anchored to the ground, allowing it to serve as a skid for the rear of the carriage. Thus, the M1 had a dual recoil system in which the barrel recoiled in its cradle while the entire carriage recoiled on the front and rear platforms.

The 35.5cm M1 howitzer was the first of the German Army's modern siege guns to see action. Used to bombard Belgian, French and Soviet fortifications, in the last years of the war the howitzers were employed as conventional long-range heavy artillery pieces. (M. Romanych)

For short-distance transport, the M1 was dismantled into six parts and loaded onto wheeled trailers towed by half-track artillery tractors. Long-distance transport was accomplished by putting the loaded trailers on flat railway wagons. A gantry crane was needed to assemble and disassemble the howitzer, which, despite its bulk, took only about two hours.

The M1 was manually operated. The barrel was elevated and set using a hand-wheel located on the top carriage. Direction of fire was adjusted in one of two ways. Fine adjustments were made using a hydraulic jack located inside the bottom carriage to lift the top carriage, allowing it to shift up to 3 degrees either side of centre. For greater changes in azimuth, the crew raised the rear end of the carriage off the ground, tilted it forward so the weight of the howitzer shifted onto the front platform, and then pivoted the howitzer on its turntable by pushing the carriage and the rear platform in one direction or the other. Other than the electric-powered ammunition winch, loading operations were done manually.

The howitzer fired a 575kg anti-concrete projectile. Rate of fire was one round every four minutes and maximum range was 20,850m. Ammunition was always in short supply. Some 2,800 rounds were ordered in 1940, but

The crew of the M1 howitzer could quickly assemble the gun in two hours by using an electric-powered gantry crane to lift the howitzer's components off trailers and set them in place on the firing position. This trailer is carrying the gun's bottom carriage and rear platform. (G. Heuer)

The 28cm Haubitze L/12 was built in the 1890s for use against armoured battleships. Twelve of the guns were mounted on the Westwall as heavy artillery in 1939. This howitzer of Stellungs Artillerie Abteilung 799 is in a fortified artillery position near Welmlingen, Germany. (M. Romanych)

only 300 were produced per month and rarely were more than 200 rounds available per gun. In 1943, a Röchling projectile (see below) was developed for the M1 but was it never used in combat.

World War I-Era Guns

In 1938, the German Army brought 16 obsolete 28cm coastal defence artillery pieces back into service as static heavy artillery on the Westwall. The guns, built by Krupp, were among the few types of large-calibre artillery pieces Germany was allowed to keep under the Versailles Treaty. Two models of 28cm guns were returned to service – the 28cm Haubitze L/12 (28cm howitzer with a barrel length of 12 calibres) and the 28cm Küstenhaubitze (coastal howitzer) L/12. Despite their designation as howitzers, both guns were short-barrelled mortars. The 28cm Haubitze, which entered service in 1892, was a foundation gun designed to be permanently mounted in a concrete coastal battery. The gun's carriage was a large, boxy steel beam-and-sheet metal structure mounted on a 360-degree turntable. The recoil system was an old-style gravity mechanism that absorbed recoil by moving the barrel and cradle up an inclined plane. During World War I, 37 28cm guns were mounted to coastal artillery batteries. The Versailles Treaty permitted Germany to keep 17 of the guns for coastal defence. The 28cm Küstenhaubitze, which entered service in 1907, was a modernized version of the 28cm Haubitze. It was smaller, lighter and had a more efficient recoil system. Twenty-eight of the guns were used as coastal artillery during World War I, with 13 pieces surviving post-war destruction by the Allies.

Although not designed as siege artillery, the 28cm guns eventually fell into that role. Before returning to service in 1939, the guns were refurbished and underwent a few minor modifications. Both versions had a range of 11,400m and rate of fire of one round every four minutes. Although several types of projectiles were originally manufactured for the guns, in 1940 only a high-explosive round was available. By early 1940, 12 28cm Haubitze and three 28cm Küstenhaubitze pieces were installed on the Westwall. After the defeat of France, the guns were put in storage until they were sent to the Eastern Front in 1942 as siege artillery. To move the guns, each was

THE 35.5CM M1 HOWITZER

The M1 howitzer stood 5.5m tall and weighed 78 metric tonnes. Its 35.5cm calibre was unique, being the only artillery piece manufactured for the army in that bore size. To move, the howitzer was disassembled into six pieces – barrel, cradle, breech block, top carriage, bottom carriage and front platform – carried on wheeled trailers and towed by half-track artillery tractors. A seventh tractor towed a trailer with the gantry crane. For long-distance transport, the loaded trailers, artillery tractors and other battery equipment were loaded onto standard flat railway cars.

Under ideal conditions, assembly took two hours. After the firing position was cleared and levelled, steel rails were placed on the ground and the gantry crane was erected and set on the rails. The crane had wheels so it could move back and forth on the rails to lift the howitzer's components from their trailers and set them in place. First, the front platform and turntable were unloaded, set into position and staked to the ground. Next, the rear platform trailer was pulled into position under the gantry crane, the platform was unloaded and attached to the turntable. Then the bottom carriage was unloaded and set on the turntable. In similar manner, the top carriage, cradle and barrel were unloaded in turn and added to the assembly. As the howitzer took shape, the ladders and crew platform were put in place so the crew could climb onto the gun. Lastly, the munitions winch, loading tray and rammer were placed on the crew platform and the howitzer was function-checked for proper operation.

Components of the M1 Howitzer

1. Front platform with turntable

2. Bottom carriage and rear platform

3. Top carriage with crew platform

4. Cradle

5. Barrel

6. Breech block

7. Rear platform

M1 Howitzer on Road Trailers

A. Crane

B. Front platform with turntable

C. Bottom carriage and rear platform

D. Top carriage with crew platform

E. Cradle

F. Barrel

G. Breech block

Three pre-World War I-vintage 28cm Küstenhaubitze L/12 coastal artillery pieces were returned to service in 1939 for use on the Westwall. This gun is mounted to a concrete firing position at the Jüterbog firing range. (M. Rupp)

disassembled into four loads – barrel, cradle, carriage and turntable, and foundation – using cranes and winches, then loaded onto special three-axle trailers. For rail transport, the guns' components were loaded onto standard flatbed railway wagons. In the field, the gun was mounted on a timber beam foundation laid into a pit in the ground. Up to four days were needed to assemble and emplace the gun for firing.

The German Army also rebuilt a World War I 42cm Gamma-Gerät howitzer. The gun, designed by Krupp in 1906 and fielded in 1911, was used during World War I against Belgian, French and Russian forts. It is not certain whether the gun escaped post-war destruction by being dismantled and hidden or if it was rebuilt from spare parts on hand at the Krupp factory. Either way, in 1937 the 42cm Gamma howitzer was assembled and refurbished by Krupp for use as a test gun for concrete-penetrating rounds at Krupp's Meppen range. The differences between the original and the rebuilt versions of the gun were minor, although the rebuilt version had no spare barrels. Like the 28cm coastal guns, the 42cm Gamma was a platform gun suited for positional rather than manoeuvre warfare. Weighing 140 metric tonnes, it fired from a metal foundation placed in a pit dug into the ground. The gun could only be moved by rail. For transport, it was disassembled into seven loads and placed on flatbed railway wagons using a gantry crane. Emplacement and assembly took at least 24 hours. Though old technology, the gun had a long range of 15,000m and its 1,215kg anti-concrete projectile was capable of penetrating more than 3m of reinforced concrete.

The World War I-vintage 42cm Gamma howitzer was reconstructed and brought into service when the German Army realized that the new Karl mortars and Gustav-Gerät railway gun would not be ready in time for the invasion of Belgium and France. (NARA)

Emplacing super-heavy siege artillery pieces entailed hard manual labour. Here, soldiers of schwere Artillerie Abteilung 800 are preparing the unit's 42cm Gamma howitzer for action against the Maginot Line in June 1940. (M. Romanych)

Skoda Siege Guns

After World War I, Austria retained two 30.5cm mortars and one 38cm howitzer. These guns were taken by the German Army when Austria united with Germany in 1938 (although the 38cm howitzer was not put into service). Six months later, after the annexation of the Sudetenland, Germany purchased 17 30.5cm mortars from Czechoslovakia and then, after the remainder of the country was occupied in 1939, the German Army acquired a few more 30.5cm mortars and one 42cm howitzer. These old artillery pieces, while smaller in calibre than the new generation of super-heavy guns produced by Krupp and Rheinmetall, were a windfall because they were

The World War I-vintage Skoda-built 30.5cm Mörser (t) was the most versatile siege gun used by the German Army. This mortar of schwere Artillerie Abteilung 641 is in position near Longuyon, France, for shelling the Maginot Line fortress of Fermont on 21 June 1940. (M. Romanych)

All aspects of emplacing and operating the 30.5cm Mörser (t) were done manually. Here the crew is using hand jacks to lower the gun's carriage and gun cradle onto its foundation. (M. Romanych)

combat-proven and came with an ample supply of spare parts and ammunition.

The most numerous siege gun in German service was the 30.5cm Mörser Model 16 (or just M.16). The first version of the mortar, the 30.5cm Mörser M.11, was fielded with the Austro-Hungarian Army in 1912 and used effectively during World War I against Belgian, French, Russian and Italian forts. The success of the M.11 mortar led to the manufacture of an upgraded version, the 30.5cm Mörser M.11/16, and then the even better 30.5cm Mörser M.16. In total, the Austro-Hungarian Army had 101 30.5cm mortars during the war (44 M.11s, 28 M.11/16s and 29 M.16s), of which the M.16 mortars remained in service with the post-war Czechoslovakian Army and were subsequently acquired by the German Army. Without the Skoda 30.5cm mortars, the German Army would have had no siege artillery at the start of the war. In 1944, the German Army captured several Skoda siege guns from the Italian Army, but none were put into use.

By 1939, the German Army had 23 30.5cm M.16 mortars, which it redesignated as the 30.5cm Mörser (t) (t: *tschechisch*, or Czechoslovakian). The 30.5cm mortar was a 35-tonne foundation gun, but was relatively mobile and quick to emplace. For transport, it was easily disassembled into three components – barrel, carriage (with cradle) and foundation (with turntable) – and carried on trailers towed by wheeled or half-track artillery

E

THE 30.5CM MORTAR IN ACTION

The World War I-vintage Skoda-built 30.5cm mortar, designated as the 30.5cm Mörser (t) by the German Army, was the workhorse of World War II German siege artillery. The German Army acquired 23 of the mortars from Czechoslovakia and used them throughout the war as both siege and heavy artillery. Overall, the 30.5cm mortar – with its robust design, ease of use and mobility, and abundant stock of ammunition – was the best siege gun used by the German Army.

When in action, the mortar was typically emplaced behind a forest or hill to hide its position from enemy observation. The ideal position had easy access from a road, level ground for emplacement of the mortars and concealment for the accompanying vehicles and equipment. Firing operations were conducted in assembly-line fashion. The ammunition was prepared in a nearby supply point where the projectiles were uncrated, inspected and fuzed and the cartridge cases were primed and packed with propellant charges. Projectiles were delivered to the mortars on a handcart, while the cartridge cases were carried by soldiers.

The mortar could fire one round every five minutes. A crew of ten to twelve soldiers operated the gun. The crew loaded the mortar by manually sliding a projectile from the handcart onto the loading tray and then using a ramrod to push the projectile from the loading tray into the barrel. Next, the cartridge case was seated in the breech behind the projectile, and the breech block was closed. The mortar's barrel was elevated to the proper angle for firing, and the crew moved away from the gun to avoid the shock of the muzzle blast. The gun was fired by a soldier pulling on a lanyard that activated the firing mechanism. After the gun fired, the breech block was opened and the cartridge case was extracted.

tractors. No crane was needed to assemble the mortar. Six to eight hours were needed for emplacement. First a pit was dug for the mortar's foundation. The foundation was then offloaded from its trailer and lowered into the pit. The carriage trailer was brought into position, lifted from its trailer using the hand jacks and then lowered onto the foundation and bolted to the turntable. Next, the barrel trailer was towed into place next to the carriage. Block and tackle were used to pull the barrel off the trailer and slide it into the cradle on the gun carriage. With assembly completed, the firing site was cleared of equipment and materiel and the gun was function checked. Although the mortar was manually operated, it could fire one round every five minutes. Maximum range was 12,300m. Its anti-fortification projectile could penetrate 2m of reinforced concrete.

In 1939, the German Army purchased a 42cm Autohaubitze M.17 from Skoda. The howitzer was refurbished in the autumn of 1939 and brought into service for the invasion of France as the 42cm Haubitze (t). Like the 30.5cm mortar, the 42cm Haubitze was a World War I design. The first version of the howitzer was built as a turret-mounted coastal defence gun, but soon after war broke out in 1914, three of the howitzers were dismounted and sent to support the field army. The howitzers performed well, so Skoda built a road-transportable version called the 42cm Autohaubitze M.16 and in 1917 began manufacturing an improved version, the 42cm Autohaubitze M.17. When the war ended, one M17 was at the front and several were in construction at Skoda's Pilsen factory, where they remained until one was purchased by the German Army in 1939.

The 42cm howitzer was much larger, heavier (105 metric tonnes) and less mobile than the 30.5cm mortar, but it packed a much bigger punch and had longer range (14,100m). To accommodate the force of the barrel's recoil, the gun had a more robust carriage, an improved recoil system and a massive steel box foundation measuring 6.5m long, 5.2m wide and 1.6m tall. A 360-degree turntable built into the foundation and a narrow-gauge track with hand carts was used to deliver projectiles to the howitzer. Emplacing the 42cm howitzer was similar to the 30.5cm mortar, except much more time was needed to dig the pit for the foundation and assemble the howitzer. For transport, the howitzer was disassembled into four loads – barrel, carriage and the two foundation halves. The barrel and two foundation pieces were carried on heavy-duty wheeled trailers, while the gun carriage served as its own trailer by attaching wheeled limbers to the front and rear of the carriage. Half-track artillery tractors were used to tow the trailers. Despite its bulk, the 42cm howitzer was loaded and operated by hand. It fired the same anti-concrete projectile as Krupp's 42cm Gamma and had a rate of fire of one round every five minutes. A serious limitation of the 42cm howitzer was that it had no spare barrel; once worn out, the gun was useless.

Only one 42cm Haubitze (t) was used by the German Army. Here it is seen during a lull in the shelling of the Maginot Line in the Vosges Mountains in June 1940. A 1-tonne shell is ready to be rammed into the breech and the cartridge case containing bagged propellant is also at the ready. (M. Rupp)

Soldiers of schwere Artillerie Abteilung 800 emplacing the unit's 42cm Haubitze (t) near Oberotterbach, Germany, in late June 1940. One half of the howitzer's foundation is being lifted off its trailer for placement into the foundation pit. (M. Rupp)

German-Built Siege Guns

Nomenclature	Type	Manufacturer	Year Fielded[1]	Number[2]	Maximum Range (m)
28cm Haubitze L/12	Mortar	Krupp	1892/1939	12	11,400
28cm Küstenhaubitze L/12	Mortar	Krupp	1907/1939	3	11,400
35.5cm Haubitze M1	Howitzer	Rheinmetall-Borsig	1939	8	20,850
42cm Gamma-Gerät	Howitzer	Krupp	1911/1940	1	15,000
54cm Gerät 041 'Karl-Gerät'	Howitzer	Rheinmetall-Borsig	1944	3[3]	10,000
60cm Gerät 040 'Karl-Gerät'	Mortar	Rheinmetall-Borsig	1941	6	4,300
80cm Kanone (E) 'Gustav-Gerät'	Railway Gun	Krupp	1942	2	48,000
Foreign-Built Siege Guns					
30.5cm Mörser (t)	Mortar	Skoda	1916/1939	23	12,300
42cm Haubitze (t)	Howitzer	Skoda	1918/1940	1	14,100

Notes:

(1) When two dates are listed, the first is the year when the gun was fielded, and the second is when it was returned to service with the German Army during World War II.

(2) The number of guns used by the German Army during World War II.

(3) One 54cm Gerät 041 was manufactured and two Gerät 040s were converted to Gerät 041.

Ammunition

Ammunition for the siege guns consisted of two parts – the projectile and cartridge case. The projectiles for the 54cm Gerät 041, 60cm Gerät 040, 35.5cm M1, 42cm Gamma, Skoda 42cm howitzer and 80cm 'Gustav-Gerät' were concrete-penetrating rounds. These projectiles had a blunt, hardened steel nose that allowed the projectile to burrow deep into reinforced concrete before detonating. A ballistic cap was fitted to the shell's nose to improve the aerodynamics of the shell during flight. The Skoda 30.5cm mortar fired an armour-piercing round with a hardened nose designed prior to World War I to penetrate masonry or concrete fortifications. The old Krupp 28cm coastal guns fired World War I-era rounds that had been made for use against armoured ships. These rounds had a thick, hardened nose and were fuzed to detonate after penetrating the deck armour of a ship.

The 60cm Karl-Gerät anti-concrete round was typical of the projectiles fired by most German siege guns. The round weighed 1,270kg, was filled with a 280kg explosive charge and had a blunt, hardened steel nose (note: this round is missing its ballistic cap). (M. Romanych)

Of the various types of anti-fortification projectiles, these had the least penetrative power against reinforced concrete and were more suited for use as conventional high-explosive rounds. Two siege guns – the Skoda 30.5cm mortar and the 80cm 'Gustav-Gerät' – also had a conventional high-explosive projectile. The cartridge case held the propellant charges and the primer for igniting the propellant. Propellant charges were bagged in increments, so the amount of propellant placed in the cartridge case could be adjusted to vary the trajectory of the rounds.

In the 1930s, a special projectile was designed by Röchling'sche Eisen- und Stahlwerke specifically for use against concrete fortifications. The 'Röchling' shell was a slender sub-calibre, dart-shaped, fin-stabilized projectile. Made of dense steel, the projectile concentrated its mass on a much smaller area of the target than conventional rounds and was thus able to achieve greater penetration. In 1940, work began on shells for a 21cm howitzer, and in 1943, projectiles were developed for the 35.5cm M1 howitzer. As many as 200 rounds were manufactured for the M1, some of which were test-fired on the former Belgian Fort Battice at Liège. The projectiles achieved exceptionally high penetration – up to 4.2m of reinforced concrete – but were not very accurate due to problems with stability of the shell in flight. Röchling projectiles were never used in combat.

OPERATIONAL HISTORY

Siege Gun Units

The siege guns used cartridge cases to hold propellant charges and prevent gases leaking from the breech when the gun was fired. These bagged propellant charges for the 30.5cm Mörser (t) came in four sizes, ranging from 1.17 to 1.8kg. (NARA)

The basic siege gun unit was the *schwere Artillerie Batterie* (heavy artillery battery). Batteries equipped with 28cm and 30.5cm artillery pieces typically had two guns. Although independent batteries were not uncommon, two or three batteries were organized into a *schwere Artillerie Abteilung* (heavy artillery battalion) when possible. Early in the war, siege gun and heavy artillery batteries were often assigned to the same battalion, forming a mixed artillery battalion that could bombard permanent fortifications and provide heavy artillery support. Units equipped with the larger-calibre 35.5cm M1, 42cm Gamma and Skoda guns, 60cm Karl mortars and the 80cm Dora were unique organisations, tailored to meet the specific technical and operational requirements of their artillery pieces. When in the field, siege gun units were allocated to army groups or armies, which in turn assigned the units to a corps or division for a specific operation.

1939 – Poland

When war began, the only super-heavy guns available to the German Army for siege operations were Skoda 30.5cm mortars. Five batteries, with two mortars each, were mobilized for the invasion of Poland. Four batteries were assigned to Artillerie Abteilungen (Art.Abt.) 624 and 641 to support Army Group South. Each battalion had one battery of 10cm heavy cannons and two batteries of 30.5cm mortars. Art.Abt. 624 was assigned to the Tenth Army for its advance on Warsaw and Art.Abt. 641 to the Fourteenth Army to attack Fortress Krakow. The fifth battery, named Mörser Batterie Deck after the commander of the battery, was assigned to Army Group North's Third Army to bombard Fortress Graudenz (modern Grudziądz) in the Pomeranian (Polish) Corridor.

Mörser Batterie Deck was the first siege gun battery to go into action. On the first day of the invasion the battery's mortars, and 11 batteries of heavy artillery, bombarded Graudenz's fortifications. After three days of combat, the fortress fell on 4 September, and Batterie Deck redeployed to support an attack on Fortress Modlin (known as Novogeorgievsk during World War I). There, along with 12 batteries of heavy artillery, the battery shelled forts on the northern side of the fortress for a week from 13–19 September. Although several ring forts were captured, the fortress's garrison held firm, and the attack was suspended when the Third Army with its artillery was ordered to end the attack and encircle the northern side of Warsaw. Meanwhile, in southern and central Poland, Art.Abt. 624 and 641 saw little action because the Polish border fortifications were quickly overrun and the fortresses at Kraków and Deblin (known as Ivanograd in World War I) were captured without a fight.

As Army Group South approached Warsaw, one 30.5cm battery of Art. Abt. 641 remained with the Fourteenth Army for its attack on Fortress Przemyśl while the rest of the battalion joined the Eighth Army for the final assault on Warsaw. The bombardment of the Polish defences began on 22 September and lasted for six days until the 27th. Batterie Deck supported the Third Army's attack on the north side of Warsaw, while

The only siege guns employed during the campaign in Poland were ten 30.5cm mortars. Ironically, the mortars, which were designed during World War I, were primarily used to bombard Great War-vintage fortifications at Graudenz, Modlin, Przemyśl and Warsaw. (NARA)

Art.Abt. 641 supported the Eighth Army on the western and southern sides of the city. The two mortar batteries shelled the ring forts, but then, as the forts were captured, the mortars shifted fire to civilian targets within the city. As the fight for Warsaw ended, the siege guns returned to Fortress Modlin and bombarded its forts until the garrison surrendered on 29 September.

1940 – Campaign in the West

Ten siege gun batteries equipped with 18 guns (16 30.5cm mortars, one 35.5cm M1 howitzer and one 42cm Gamma howitzer) were allocated for the campaign in the West. The batteries were all assigned to Army Group B's Sixth Army opposite the Belgium fortifications at Liège. Their organization was as follows: schwere Artillerie Abteilungen (schw.Art.Abt.) 624 and 641 each had two batteries of 30.5cm mortars plus a battery of 21cm guns; schw.Art.Abt. 815 had three 30.5cm mortar batteries; schw.Art.Abt. 800 had Battery 779 with two 30.5cm mortars, Batterie 810 with the 35.5cm M1 and Batterie 820 with the 42cm Gamma howitzer. During the campaign, after

CONCEPT AND PROTOTYPE GUNS

During the war, artillery manufacturers Rheinmetall, Krupp and Skoda (which was integrated into the German armaments industry after the occupation of Czechoslovakia) proposed and designed several siege artillery pieces. In general, each development project sought greater mobility and range for the guns. Many of the concepts were either technically or tactically impractical.

Rheinmetall designed two variants of the self-propelled Karl mortar, one that mated the 24cm Kanone 3 and another the 35.5cm gun M1 howitzer to the tracked carrier. Allied bombing destroyed the 35.5cm prototype, while the 24cm variant, known as the K4F, was completed but not put into production.

Krupp, while designing the 80cm Gustav-Gerät railway gun in the 1930s, considered several variants of the gun. A self-propelled version called the ER-Gerät X3 was similar in appearance to the Gustav-Gerät, but had a different carriage structure, powered tracked suspension systems instead of the four railway bogie units, and an engine and drivetrain to propel the gun over ground. Design work on these variants ended when war began, though discussion about building a self-propelled version of the Gustav-Gerät reappeared as late as 1943.

Skoda's designs were more practical. Under German direction, the firm created several designs for 30.5cm and 42cm calibre mortars and howitzers in both towed and self-propelled configurations, including a 42cm mortar mounted on a modified Tiger II tank chassis. Of these designs, only two entered the manufacturing process – a towed 42cm howitzer that was destroyed by Allied bombing before it was assembled and a prototype towed 30.5cm heavy mortar that was captured by the US Army.

1. Rheinmetall Self-Propelled 35.5cm Howitzer: This design mounted an M1 Howitzer minus its lower carriage and firing platform onto a Karl mortar tracked carrier. The gun's carriage was modified to fit into the hull of the carrier and rest on a roller recoil mechanism much like that of the 60cm Karl mortar. Range and rate of fire were the same as for the M1 howitzer. A prototype of the howitzer was being manufactured until it was destroyed by Allied bombing of Rheinmetall's main factory in Düsseldorf.

2. Skoda 30.5cm Heavy Mortar: In the last months of the war Skoda manufactured a mobile 30.5cm heavy mortar. Design of the mortar commenced in January 1945 and the prototype was completed in early April 1945, but was never fielded. The mortar had a smoothbore barrel mounted on a carriage similar to Skoda's other heavy artillery pieces. Even though the gun had a long barrel, it was classified as a mortar because of its steep angle of fire and type of projectile. The carriage was mounted on a circular pedestal upon which the gun could traverse 360 degrees. A skid mounted to the rear of the carriage provided stability. The mortar had two types of fin-stabilized projectiles: a light 160kg shell and a heavy 235kg shell. The mortar was transported in two loads – barrel and carriage – and assembled using a crane. The mortar's estimated range was 10,000m.

A 30.5cm mortar battery of Artillerie Abteilung 641 in an assembly area near Przemyśl, Poland, in mid-September 1939. The unit is equipped with Czech-built Tatra T 25 artillery tractors. (M. Romanych)

In the early years of the war, the super-heavy guns were showcased by German propaganda. This M1 howitzer, with cartridge cases at the ready, was photographed somewhere on the Westwall during the 'Phoney War' in April 1940. (M. Rupp)

Belgium fell, an eleventh battery – Battery 830 equipped with a 42cm Skoda howitzer – was sent to Army Group C for its attack against the Maginot Line.

Liège's defences were eight World War I-era forts laid out in a circular arc to protect the eastern and southern approaches to the city and a second line of four modern forts, including Fort Eben-Emael, located further east of the city near the German border. The older forts, built in the late 1800s and heavily damaged by German siege guns in 1914, were rebuilt by the Belgians after the war and armed with turret-mounted 75mm, 105mm and 150mm artillery pieces. The four modern forts, built in the mid-1930s, consisted of a central fortified redoubt surrounded by a wide defensive moat defended by casemates armed with anti-tank and machine guns. The redoubts were capped by up to 4.5m of reinforced concrete and were armed with 75mm guns mounted in armoured turrets. Two of the forts – Eben Emael and Battice – also had turret-mounted long-range 120mm guns.

Fort Eben-Emael was captured on the second day of the invasion (11 May) by airborne assault. Schwere Artillerie Abteilung 641 was positioned to provide artillery support but was not needed. The capture of the fort prompted the Belgian III Corps to withdraw from the area and allowed the German Sixth Army to bypass Liège, while detaching the 223rd Infantry Division to capture the fortifications. On 12 May, as the 223rd Infantry Division, along with the 251st Infantry Division from the Second Army, surrounded the fortress, artillery and Stukas bombarded the forts. The next day more German heavy artillery, long-range railway guns and the siege guns of schw.Art.Abt. 624, 641 and 800 arrived and began shelling the World War I-era forts on the eastern side of the fortress. The 223rd and 251st Infantry Divisions attacked and captured two of the forts on 16 May, and the remaining World War I-era forts quickly fell over the next three days. With only three forts in Belgian hands, schw.Art.Abt. 624, 641 and 800 were redeployed to

Namur, but they arrived after the fortress was captured. Meanwhile, schw. Art.Abt. 800 and Batterie 820 continued shelling Liège's remaining forts, of which one was captured on 21 May and another the following day. The last fort – Tancrémont – capitulated on 29 May, the day after the Belgian Army surrendered. Even though the siege guns fired hundreds of rounds at Liege's forts, most of the damage to the fortifications was caused by Stuka bombing, not the artillery.

The next action for the siege artillery was in Flanders near the city of Valenciennes, where the French border fortifications were bolstering the French First Army's defence against the advance of Army Group B's Sixth Army. The largest fortification was Fort de Maulde, a modern fortified artillery battery built into an old obsolete earth and masonry fort dating from the 1880s. The artillery battery consisted of a large observation block and three casemates armed with four rapid-fire 75mm guns and a long-range 155mm cannon. On 20 May, the Sixth Army's XXVII Corps placed Fort de Maulde under artillery fire. The fort returned fire and an artillery battle ensued. Schwere Artillerie Abteilung 641 arrived on 22 May to join the battle. For two days, the battalion's 21cm and 30.5cm guns shelled the fort. The bombardment heavily damaged the old fort but did little to the fortified artillery battery because the 30.5cm mortars missed the observatory and artillery casemates. Fort de Maulde's garrison held out until 27 May, abandoning the fort only as it was about to be surrounded by German infantry.

After the evacuation of British and some French forces from Dunkirk, the German Army redistributed the siege gun battalions among the Army Groups. Schwere Artillerie Abteilung 815 and Batterie 779 remained with Army Group B's Sixth Army in Flanders, schw.Art.Abt. 624 moved to Army Group A's Twelfth Army north of Reims, schw.Art.Abt. 641 was assigned to Army Group A's Sixteenth Army opposite the Maginot Line in northern Alsace and schw.Art.Abt. 800 – along with newly assigned Batterie 830 – was allocated to Army Group C's First Army along the Maginot Line in the Sarre Region.

Only one M1 howitzer was available for use during the 1940 campaign in the West. Built to deliver long-range precision fire against small fortified targets, the howitzer inexplicably fired wide on three occasions during the campaign. (M. Rupp)

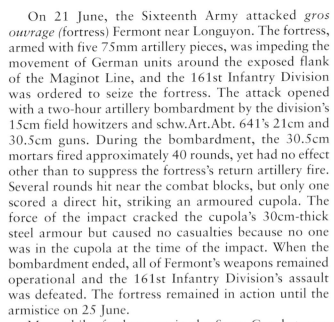

On 21 June, the Sixteenth Army attacked *gros ouvrage (*fortress) Fermont near Longuyon. The fortress, armed with five 75mm artillery pieces, was impeding the movement of German units around the exposed flank of the Maginot Line, and the 161st Infantry Division was ordered to seize the fortress. The attack opened with a two-hour artillery bombardment by the division's 15cm field howitzers and schw.Art.Abt. 641's 21cm and 30.5cm guns. During the bombardment, the 30.5cm mortars fired approximately 40 rounds, yet had no effect other than to suppress the fortress's return artillery fire. Several rounds hit near the combat blocks, but only one scored a direct hit, striking an armoured cupola. The force of the impact cracked the cupola's 30cm-thick steel armour but caused no casualties because no one was in the cupola at the time of the impact. When the bombardment ended, all of Fermont's weapons remained operational and the 161st Infantry Division's assault was defeated. The fortress remained in action until the armistice on 25 June.

The 42cm Gamma howitzer of schwere Artillerie Abteilung 800 in firing position near Hanweiler, Germany, in June 1940. The battery's officers are standing on the gun. (M. Romanych)

Meanwhile, farther east in the Sarre Gap between Metz and Lauter, three corps of the First Army attacked a weakly fortified sector of the Maginot Line. The attack was supported by about 1,000 artillery pieces, including eight batteries of long-range railway artillery and the siege guns of schw.Art.Abt. 800. This was the largest concentration of artillery during the French campaign. Schwere Artillerie Abteilung 800's 35.5cm M1, 42cm Gamma and 42cm Skoda howitzers were tasked to destroy several key casemates and blockhouses blocking the corps' avenues of advance. Ammunition was limited: only 30 rounds were available for the M1 and 22 rounds for each of the 42cm guns.

The French defences at Sarre resembled a World War I trench system, with multiple lines of trenches reinforced by field fortifications, concrete casemates and blockhouses, and belts of anti-tank and wire obstacles. Central to the defence was a series of flooded areas meant to funnel German attacks into the strongest fortifications. Manning the defences were five French machine-gun regiments supported by about 100 artillery pieces.

The German offensive began early on 14 June with a 90-minute bombardment, followed by dive-bomber attacks. The bombardment was largely ineffective because ground fog forced the artillery to fire blind. Other than the 42cm Gamma, which scored a direct hit on a concrete casemate, the guns of schw.Art.Abt. 800 missed their targets. Even the 35.5cm M1, which was designed to hit small concrete fortifications, fired wide of its targets. The rest of the barrage did little better, and the infantry attacked into nearly intact French defences. Hard fighting resulted, and by the end of the day the French defences still held. Casualties were so high that the First Army commander considered calling off the attack, but that night the French withdrew from their defensive positions, allowing the First Army to occupy the fortifications the next day.

With the conclusion of the Sarre attack, schw.Art. Abt. 800 supported two attacks against the Maginot Line in northern Alsace: one by the 215th Infantry Division in the Vosges Mountains and another by the 246th Infantry Division in the Rhine Valley. The 215th Infantry Division's area of attack was a mountainous area near Bitche, fortified by a single line of concrete casemates and blockhouses manned by French fortress infantry. Schwere Artillerie Abteilung 800 supported the division with M1 and 42cm Skoda guns. A two-hour barrage began the attack on 14 June, followed by Stuka bombing. Despite the barrage's intensity, no direct hits were scored on the fortifications. Yet the attack still went forward and by the end of the day, 22 casemates and blockhouses were captured, creating a 5km-wide gap in the French fortification line. During the battle, the nearby French artillery fortresses of Four-à-Chaux and Hochwald shelled German positions. In response, schw.Art.Abt. 800 and Stukas bombarded the fortresses, but inflicted no significant damage.

In the Rhine Valley, the 246th Infantry Division attempted to break through a casemate line in the Aschbach-Oberrödern area. The division attacked the French defences twice but was repulsed by artillery fire from fortresses at Hochwald and Schönenbourg. To suppress the fortress artillery, the First Army deployed the M1 and 42cm Skoda howitzers of schw.Art.Abt. 800 to positions near the fortresses. The batteries opened fire on 21 June, engaging Hochwald and Schönenbourg in a three-day artillery battle. The fortresses returned fire but failed to hit the siege gun positions. Likewise, the siege guns inflicted little damage on the fortresses. The M1 completely missed its targets, and of the 40 or more rounds fired by the 42cm Skoda howitzer at Schönenbourg, only 11 impacted on or near the fortress's combat blocks, and of those, just three scored direct hits. The most significant impact blasted a sizeable crater on the top of an artillery block but failed to penetrate its roof. Damage to Fortress Hochwald was superficial. Both fortresses continued to fight, surrendering only after the armistice.

As the French campaign ended, schw.Art.Abt. 624, 641 and 815 were assigned to the Army High Command reserve in the Metz area. By August, all three battalions were earmarked for the proposed invasion of England. Schwere Artillerie Abteilungen 624 and 641 were reorganized to increase firepower. Schwere Artillerie Abteilung 624 exchanged its 21cm howitzer battery for Batterie 779 (two 30.5cm mortars), while schw.Art.Abt. 641 replaced its 21cm howitzer battery with Batterie 810 (one 35.5cm M1) from schw.Art.Abt. 800. The other two batteries assigned to schw.Art.Abt. 800 – 820 and 830 – were disbanded, and the 42cm Gamma and Skoda howitzers were put into storage. With all its siege guns now gone, schw.Art.Abt. 800 was re-formed as a heavy artillery battalion with 15cm cannons.

1941 – Eastern Front

Unlike the campaign in the West, German forces invading the Soviet Union did not expect to confront strong modern permanent fortifications at the

The 42cm Skoda howitzer of schwere Artillerie Abteilung 800 near Schönau along the French border on 19 June 1940. The crew is preparing to fire on Maginot Line casemates in the Vosges Mountains. Two soldiers are working the crank to elevate the barrel into firing position. In the foreground are several cartridge cases used to hold the bagged propellant charges. (M. Romanych)

OPPOSITE
Schwere Artillerie Abteilung 800's 42cm Gamma howitzer firing on French fortifications in the Sarre sector of the Maginot Line. Designed to shell large fortifications, the howitzer was not accurate enough to hit the small casemates and blockhouses that formed the backbone of French defences in the Sarre region. (M. Romanych)

Another view of schwere Artillerie Abteilung 800's 42cm Skoda howitzer firing at Maginot Line fortifications in the Vosges Mountains. The projectile can be seen in flight at the top of the photograph. (M. Rupp)

outset of the campaign. Soviet border defences (sometimes called the Molotov Line) were a series of hastily built, lightly armed concrete casemates and earthworks grouped into strongpoints. Of greater concern to the German Army was the pre-World War I fortress at Brest-Litovsk (renamed Brest by the Soviets) and the stronger Stalin Line fortifications located inside the Soviet Union along its pre-1939 border.

For the invasion, 11 siege gun batteries with 21 guns were mobilized (16 30.5cm mortars, one M1 howitzer and four new super-heavy 60cm Karl mortars) organized into four heavy artillery battalions. The Ninth Army, located near Grodno, had schw.Art.Abt. 624 and 815, each with three 30.5cm mortar batteries, and schw.Art.Abt. 641, with a one-gun M1 howitzer battery and two 30.5cm mortar batteries. Army Group Centre's Fourth Army, which faced the Brest fortress, had schw.Art.Abt. 833, with a two-gun 60cm Karl mortar battery. The battalion's other battery was assigned to Army Group South's Seventeenth Army for an attack on a Molotov Line strongpoint near Lwów (Lemberg to the Germans).

The main action for the siege guns was at Brest. The fortress was a 19th-century, star-shaped fortification surrounded by two rings of forts located on the border between German- and Soviet-occupied Poland. At the centre of the fortress was the 'Citadel', a large fortified barracks building surrounded by a complex of earth and masonry fortifications. Encircling the Citadel were two rings of concrete forts; however, the fortifications were of minimal use to the Soviets because the forts on the western side of the ring had been occupied by the Germans since the partition of Poland in September 1939. Defending Brest were the Soviet 6th and 42nd Infantry Divisions.

The capture of Brest was assigned to the Fourth Army's XII Corps. Sixty-two heavy artillery pieces, 18 Nebelwerfer and two 60cm Karl mortars (Odin and Thor) were assembled for the bombardment. Schwere Artillerie

One of schwere Artillerie Abteilung 833's two Karl mortars receiving ammunition for shelling the Soviet fortress at Brest during the first days of Operation *Barbarossa*. (NARA)

Abteilung 833 emplaced the Karl mortars less than 2,000m from the fortress. At 0315hrs on 22 June, the artillery fired a short, intense 30-minute artillery bombardment. Thor fired only three times and Odin four, before rounds stuck in their barrels and both mortars had to stop firing for the day. Despite the barrage, the infantry assault failed to capture the fortress. On the second day, Thor fired seven rounds, but Odin malfunctioned and did not fire. The next day, Thor managed 11 rounds and Odin fired six – their last shots. In three days of shelling, the Karl mortars fired 31 of their allotted 36 rounds, yet the fortress did not fall. The fighting continued for another five days until organized Soviet resistance ended on 29 June. Post-battle reports noted that while the 60cm rounds had left large craters, no fortified works were significantly damaged by the rounds. At least two rounds were duds. However, because the Karl mortars reportedly had significantly degraded the Soviet troops' morale, the mortars were deemed a success.

Meanwhile, in Army Group South, schw.Art.Abt. 833's two other Karl mortars (Adam and Eva) supported the attack of Seventeenth Army's IV Corps on a Molotov Line strongpoint near Lwów. The position – Wielki Dzial – was a network of field works reinforced by groups of concrete infantry and artillery casemates. On 21 June, the mortars were driven from their assembly area to the firing positions. However, Eva broke a track enroute and could not participate in the battle. Adam successfully emplaced and opened fire at 0805hrs on 22 June, but after only four rounds suffered a mechanical failure and ceased firing. The infantry still assaulted and Wielki Dzial was captured the next day. The Karl mortars were no longer needed, and along with the rest of schw.Art.Abt. 833 were sent back to Germany, where the battalion was rearmed with 21cm howitzers.

After the Soviet border defences were overrun, schw.Art.Abt. 624, 641 and 815 were placed in Army Group Centre's reserve. The only recorded combat action for the battalions was from 24–26 June when schw.Art.Abt. 641 provided artillery support to VIII Corps during a Soviet counterattack in the Grodno area. At the end of June, after Army Group Centre captured Stalin Line defences in the Minsk region, all three heavy artillery battalions were transferred to Army Group South for the Sixth and Seventeenth Armies' attack on the Stalin Line near Zhitomir, and then the Sixth Army's attack on the Kiev fortified region. After Kiev fell, schw.Art.Abt. 624 and 815 remained with the Sixth Army during its advance on Kharkov, while schw. Art.Abt. 641 was transferred to the Eleventh Army in mid-September for the attack on Soviet defences at the Perekop Isthmus and Sevastopol. At the end of October, schw.Art.Abt. 815 and later schw.Art.Abt. 624 returned to Germany to have their guns refurbished.

1942 – Sevastopol and Leningrad

At the beginning of 1942, the German Army had ten 30.5cm mortars and one M1 howitzer in the field, assigned to schw.Art.Abt. 641 and 815 serving with the Eleventh Army in the Crimea. Additional siege gun units were formed for the attack on Sevastopol and sent to the Eleventh Army. In February, schw.Art.Abt. 833, which had been on the Eastern Front since August 1941 as a 21cm howitzer battalion, had one of its batteries refitted with three Karl mortars (Odin, Thor and Loki) before being sent to the Eleventh Army. The 80cm K(E) Dora railway gun was assigned to the newly formed schw.Art. Abt. 672 and sent to Russia in April. The army also returned to service its old 28cm and 42cm guns. Sixteen 28cm coastal guns were issued to Batteries 741, 742 and 743 (each with four 28cm Haubitze) and schw.Art.Abt. 744 (four 28cm Küstenhaubitze), while Batterie 458 was equipped with the 42cm Skoda howitzer and Batterie 459 with the 42cm Gamma. In April, schw.Art.Abt. 624 completed its refitting. Equipped with six 30.5cm and

G

EMPLACING THE 42CM SKODA HOWITZER

Skoda designed the first 42cm howitzer for the Austro-Hungarian Army in 1917. Only one gun – designated by the Austrian Army as the 42cm Autohaubitze M.17 – was completed by the end of World War I. After the war, the howitzer remained at the Skoda factory in Pilsen until purchased by the German Army in 1939. Refurbished and redesignated as the 42cm Haubitze (t), the howitzer first saw action during the French campaign, bombarding the Maginot fortresses of Schönenbourg and Hochwald. It was used again in 1942 during the sieges of Sevastopol and Leningrad. In early 1944, the howitzer was retired from service.

The howitzer weighed 105 metric tonnes and stood 2.1m tall. Despite its bulk, the howitzer was simple to operate and, unlike many other siege guns, did not need a crane to be assembled or emplaced. The gun was broken down into four parts for transport: barrel, carriage and two foundation halves. The barrel and foundation pieces were carried on eight-wheel trailers, while the gun carriage was moved by attaching wheeled limbers to the front and rear of the carriage.

1. Emplacing the Foundation: Emplacing the howitzer began with excavating a large pit for the howitzer's foundation. Once dug, the pit was lined with prefabricated wood walls and a floor. The foundation halves were then lifted off their trailers with hand jacks, joined together, rolled over the pit and then lowered into it using hand jacks.

2. Attaching the Carriage: Next, the howitzer was placed on the foundation. The carriage, mounted on its limbers, was pulled onto the foundation. Hand jacks attached to the carriage were used to lift it off the limbers. The limbers were removed and the carriage was lowered onto the foundation and bolted to the turntable in the foundation.

3. Installing the Barrel: The barrel was inserted into the carriage's cradle. The trailer carrying the barrel was positioned next to the rear of the carriage and a system of ropes and pulleys were used to manually move the barrel from its trailer to the cradle.

4. Preparation for Action: The loading tray and ramrod assembly were attached to the rear of the carriage and a narrow-gauge track with ammunition carts was put in place to move rounds and propellant from the ammunition supply point to the howitzer. The howitzer was then oriented in the direction of fire and inspected to ensure it was ready for action.

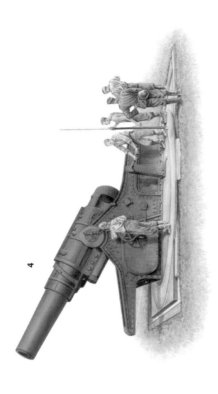

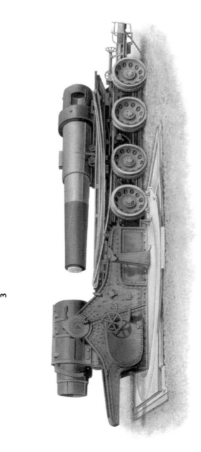

nine 21cm howitzers (a double issue of guns), the battalion returned to the front. Lastly, schw.Art.Abt. 641 received a second 35.5cm M1 howitzer. By the end of May, every siege gun unit in the German Army was with the Eleventh Army outside Sevastopol.

Preparations for the arrival of the Karl and Dora guns began in April. Schwere Artillerie Abteilung 833 dug three camouflaged firing positions south of Mamaschai on the reverse side of hills about a kilometre from the front line. Work was done at night to avoid observation and required the assistance of a combat engineer unit. The Karl mortars arrived on 20 May, off-loaded and moved to an assembly area located 3.5km from the firing positions. Construction of Dora's emplacement was far more elaborate, requiring 1,500 civilian and 1,000 Organization Todt workers, railway construction troops and other specialists. The site, located near the village of Bachtschyssaraj, took four weeks to build. During construction, a 400m-long cut was excavated through the hill that separated the marshalling yard and firing track. To hide the site from aerial observation, camouflage netting was placed to break up the outline of the gun and smoke generators were available to mask Dora's exact location. A decoy position built 4.6km away from the real firing site included a cardboard dummy of

A Karl mortar undergoing repair near Sevastopol. The mortar required frequent and extensive maintenance to ensure that both the gun and its tracked carrier were operational. (NARA)

Two M1 howitzers saw action at Sevastopol. They fired 411 rounds at Soviet fortifications but failed to inflict any significant damage. This gun is covered with camouflage netting to break up its outline. (M. Romanych)

the gun. For air defence, an anti-aircraft battalion equipped with 88mm guns was emplaced around Dora's site. Schwere Artillerie Abteilung 672 arrived at the firing site on 26 May, and in three days Dora was assembled and prepared for action.

Sevastopol was one of the strongest fortresses in the world, consisting of permanent coastal fortifications, anti-aircraft positions and three defensive lines of field fortifications for defence against land attack. The primary fortifications were ten coastal artillery batteries armed with guns ranging in calibre from 100mm to 305mm, 14 hardened anti-aircraft batteries and numerous fortified command posts and bomb-proof underground storage facilities. Of the coastal artillery batteries, the 30th and 35th Batteries (named by the Germans as 'Maxim Gorki I' and 'Maxim Gorki II'), located north and south of the harbour respectively, were particularly formidable. Each battery had four 305mm battleship guns mounted in rotating armoured turrets. Defending the fortress were army and navy troops from seven divisions, three naval brigades and various other regiments and battalion formations under the command of the Independent Coastal Army.

The Eleventh Army had three corps and more than 600 heavy and super-heavy artillery pieces, including two 28cm railway guns and 39 siege guns. The offensive began on 2 June with a five-day preparatory artillery and aerial bombardment. The 28cm and 30.5cm guns fired about 85 per cent of the total siege gun rounds, primarily shelling fortified strongpoints close to the front lines. The 35.5cm, 42cm and 80cm guns did not join the bombardment until 5 June. Dora's first shot was at Maxim Gorki I, followed by eight rounds at a coastal battery located near the harbour, and then six rounds at Fort Stalin (a fortified anti-aircraft position). All rounds missed the targets. On 6 June, the last day of the preparatory bombardment, the Karl mortars opened fire for the first time. Thor fired 16 rounds at Maxim

At Sevastopol, the 42cm Skoda howitzer fired 192 shells at Soviet fortified positions. Like other siege guns, the howitzer had a large muzzle blast that was vulnerable to detection by Soviet artillery observers. (M. Rupp)

The 80cm Dora railway gun fired 48 rounds during the siege of Sevastopol. Here, Dora is being loaded while on its firing track. In the background is a railway cut through the hill that separated the firing track from the railyard where the gun was assembled. (©Imperial War Museum (MH 862)

Gorki I from a range of 3,700m. One round hit and severely damaged an armoured turret, killing some of the crew. The other 15 rounds did not cause any significant damage. Meanwhile, Dora fired seven rounds at Fort Molotov (another fortified anti-aircraft position) and then nine at an underground ammunition dump near the harbour. No rounds hit their target.

On 7 June, the artillery fired an intense barrage in support of the ground assault. The Karl mortars fired 54 rounds at Maxim Gorki I, but only two rounds hit and the battery remained operational. Dora fired seven rounds at the ammunition dump near the harbour, where a direct hit destroyed it in a huge explosion. Other siege guns had more success bombarding Soviet infantry and artillery strongpoints.

The fighting for Sevastopol lasted another 27 days until 4 July. The siege artillery continued to shell Soviet fortifications, although the intensity slackened off as ammunition stocks were depleted. Only the 30.5cm mortars, 28cm howitzers and 35.5cm M1 had enough ammunition for the entire

Schwere Artillerie Abteilung 833 had three Karl mortars at Sevastopol, one of which, Odin, is shown here. Firing positions for the mortars were dug into the reverse slope of a hill to prevent direct observation by Soviet artillery observers. In the foreground is an aiming circle for laying the gun into position. (M. Romanych)

60cm Karl mortar Thor at Sevastopol in June 1942. Under ideal conditions, Karl mortars could fire up to six rounds an hour, but the actual rate of fire during battle was much slower. (M. Romanych)

battle. The Karl mortars fired their last rounds on 9 June, followed by the 42cm Gamma and Skoda howitzers on 13 June. Dora's last two targets were Fort Sibirien (a fortified anti-aircraft position) on 11 June and Maxim Gorki I on 17 June. Three of Dora's five rounds hit Fort Sibirien, but no significant damage was recorded. Dora fired its last five rounds at Maxim Gorki I and all rounds missed the target. The constant firing took its toll on the 28cm guns. Ten pieces (eight Haubitze and two Küstenhaubitze) were destroyed due to ruptures caused by rounds exploding in the barrels. One 28cm howitzer was also destroyed by Soviet artillery fire, while the cardboard dummy of Dora was destroyed by an air attack, but otherwise the Soviets were unable to accurately identify German siege gun positions.

During the battle, the siege artillery fired 9,006 rounds. The majority were fired by the 28cm and 30.5cm guns, which fired 3,500 and 4,920 rounds respectively. Dora fired 48 rounds, the Karl mortars 197, the 42cm Skoda howitzer 192, the 42cm Gamma 188 and the 35.5.cm M1 411. Despite thousands of rounds fired, the siege guns failed to destroy any of the Soviets' permanent fortifications, including the main target, Maxim Gorki I. Especially disappointing was the performance of the Karl and Dora guns. The Karl mortars suffered from frequent technical failures and fired a high percentage of dud rounds, while only ten of Dora's rounds landed within 60m of their target.

After the fall of Sevastopol, the Eleventh Army and its siege artillery was transferred to Army Group North for an offensive against Leningrad. En route, several siege gun units were reorganized or refitted. Batteries 741, 742 and 743 were disbanded and their remaining 28cm guns given to Batterie 744, which then had four 28cm Haubitze and one 28cm Küstenhaubitze. Schwere Artillery Abteilung 624's six 30.5cm mortars and schw.Art.Abt. 833's Karl mortars were returned to Germany for repair. In July, a new Karl mortar unit was formed – Batterie 628 with two 60cm mortars – and deployed to Army Group North. Twenty-eight siege guns were assigned to Eleventh Army for its attack on Leningrad. The siege artillery, including Dora, established firing positions, but the attack, scheduled for 23 August, was postponed and then cancelled when the Soviets launched their own offensive in the Leningrad region. During the battle, which lasted until October, the 28cm, 30.5cm,

35.5cm and 42cm guns were employed as corps-level heavy artillery. The Karl mortars and Dora did not fire a single shot and were returned to Germany. In November, when the Eleventh Army headquarters was sent to Stalingrad, the siege guns were reassigned to the Eighteenth Army.

1943–45 – Decline of the Siege Guns

During 1943, all active siege artillery units were operating with the Eighteenth Army. The older siege guns, now showing their age and running out of ammunition, were gradually replaced by heavy artillery pieces. The first guns retired were Batterie 744's 28cm howitzers which, because of continued barrel bursts, were replaced in the spring by 24cm howitzers. In the autumn, schw.Art. Abt. 641, followed by schw.Art.Abt. 624 and 815, were issued heavy artillery, including captured French pieces, which they operated alongside the siege guns until the 30.5cm mortars were pulled from the front in the summer of 1944. Additionally, after running out of ammunition, schw.Art.Abt. 641's M1 howitzers were withdrawn at the end of 1943.

Sixteen 28cm coastal guns were sent to the Eastern Front in 1942. The guns served at Sevastopol and Leningrad, but overuse resulted in numerous barrel bursts. In early 1943, the remaining operational pieces were taken out of service. (M. Romanych)

Meanwhile in Germany, the Dora and Karl guns were repaired and refitted. Gustav underwent acceptance firing and then, along with Dora, was dismantled and put into storage for the rest of the war. In August, the possibility of employing Dora and Gustav in the cross-Channel shelling of targets in south-east England was briefly considered, but not acted upon.

In May 1943, Batterie 628 was expanded to a battalion – schw.Art.Abt. 628 – equipped with three Karl mortars and sent to the Eighteenth Army to attack the Krasnaya Gorka coastal artillery fortress inside the Oranienbaum Pocket near Leningrad. Krasnaya Gorka was a coastal artillery fortress armed with 24 long-range artillery pieces. The battalion arrived in June, but because the attack was cancelled, schw.Art.Abt. 628 returned to Germany in August, put its mortars in storage and reorganized as a 21cm gun battalion.

In the first half of 1944, both 42cm siege guns were taken out of service. Batterie 458's 42cm Skoda howitzer, whose barrel had worn out during the winter of 1943/44, was armed with captured French heavy artillery pieces, and Batterie 459's 42cm Gamma howitzer was sent to Hillersleben to serve as a test gun, replaced by three French railway guns.

During the Warsaw Uprising in the summer of 1944, four Karl mortars were used to bombard positions held by Polish resistance fighters. In August, Batterie 638 was formed with Karl mortar Ziu, and sent to the Ninth Army. The battery's employment was deemed a success, even though its mortar fired several dud rounds, had a mechanical failure and had to be replaced by Loki. In September, a second unit – Batterie 428 – with Karl mortars Adam and Thor was sent to join Batterie 638. As the fight for Warsaw concluded, Batteries 638 and 428 were transferred at the end of the month to Army Group South for use at Budapest in anticipation of an uprising. The batteries arrived in mid-October, stayed for less than a week without firing a shot, and then returned to Warsaw at the end of the month. Both batteries were back at the Army base at Jüterbog in north-eastern Germany by mid-November in preparation for an offensive on the Western Front.

Six batteries with 15 siege guns were allocated for the Ardennes offensive. The batteries were assigned to the Fifth and Sixth Panzer Armies: Batteries 1100 and 1119, each with three 30.5cm mortars; Batteries 1098 and 1099, each with three M1 howitzers; Batterie 428, with Karl mortars Eva and Ziu; and Batterie 638, with Thor, which was now a 54cm Gerät 041. Both Karl batteries were not ready when the offensive began on 16 December and were further delayed en route. While in transit, Eva was damaged by an Allied aerial attack. The batteries finally arrived near the front at the end of the month, well after the offensive had stalled, and were diverted to the First Army for its offensive in northern Alsace and Lorraine. Batterie 638 was assigned to the XIII SS Corps' attack on American-held Maginot fortifications near Rohrbach, and Batterie 428 to the LXXXIX Corps for an attack towards Strasbourg. Once again, the batteries did not participate in combat because rail transit was disrupted. In January, after Batterie 638's mortar was damaged by Allied aircraft, the unit was sent back to Jüterbog, while Batterie 428 remained with the First Army.

The last action for the siege artillery occurred in March 1945. Battery 638 was refitted with a 54cm Gerät 041 (Loki) and ordered to join Army Group Weichsel east of Berlin. When the US First Army captured the Rhine River bridge at Remagen, the unit, along with Batterie 428, was sent to shell the bridge. Batterie 638 took position on 20 March and fired 14 rounds into the bridgehead until its mortar had a mechanical failure. Batterie 428 did not get to Remagen and was rerouted south to the First Army. In April, Battery 638 was disbanded and its personnel incorporated into Battery 428, which abandoned the mortars during the last weeks of the war. One 60cm Gerät 040 and two 54cm Gerät 041 pieces were captured by the US Army, one of which was sent to back to the United States, where it was later scrapped. Three 60cm Gerät 040 and one 54cm Gerät 041 pieces were captured by the Soviet Army. Today, one of the 60cm Karl mortars is in the Kubinka Tank Museum near Moscow.

The German Army built and operated siege guns right up until the last weeks of the war. These three 54cm Gerät 041 howitzers were manufactured in late 1944 by replacing barrels on existing 60cm Gerät 040 mortars. (G. Heuer)

The US Army captured the Dora and Gustav railway guns; both were disassembled and heavily damaged. Dora was discovered in Auerswalde, where it was stored since leaving Leningrad in late 1943. Located in the soon-to-be Soviet zone of occupation, Dora was subsequently turned over to the Soviet Army. Gustav was found in pieces, spread out over several kilometres of railway track near Grafenwöhr. These guns were scrapped in the 1950s and 1960s, and all that remains today are a few projectiles, cartridge cases and ammunition railway wagons located in various museums in Europe and the United States.

None of the 35.5cm M1 or Skoda 30.5cm and 42cm siege guns used by the German Army exist today, although World War I versions of the Skoda guns are in military museums in Bucharest, Hungary; Rovereto, Italy; and Belgrade, Serbia.

CONCLUSION

The performance of Krupp and Rheinmetall's super-heavy siege guns did not justify the enormous effort and resources expended for their manufacture. In battle, the guns failed to destroy or force the surrender of a single modern fortification. The 35.5cm M1 howitzer, specifically built to deliver accurate long-range shells, often fired wide of its target, a problem that the gun could ill-afford because of its limited ammunition supply. The 60cm Karl mortars' short range, frequent malfunctions and dud rounds, as well as their wide dispersion of fire, greatly limited their effectiveness. Even the few hits that the mortars scored failed to inflict decisive damage or destruction. While a technological wonder, the Dora railway gun was far too cumbersome to employ because of its massive size, and even with close spotting of the rounds, its fire was wildly inaccurate. During its short 13-day operational

This 54cm Gerät 041 Loki of Artillerie Battery 638 was captured on its railway transporter by the US First Army in April 1945. The gun shelled the Remagen Bridge over the Rhine on 20 March 1945 until it suffered a mechanical failure. Soon thereafter the mortar was abandoned and sabotaged by its crew. (NARA)

In October 1943, the 80cm Dora railway gun was put into storage at the train station in Auerswalde, near Chemnitz, where it remained until it was captured by the US Army on 14 April 1945. The day before its capture, the German 676th Engineer Battalion blew up the gun, leaving it in ruins. Seen here is a section of the gun's barrel on its railway transport wagons. (NARA)

life, Dora fired 48 rounds, at six targets, and destroyed only one, which was a subterranean ammunition depot and not a fortification.

The World War I-era guns, particularly the Skoda 30.5cm mortars, performed better than the new super-heavy guns, but only when used as heavy, not siege, artillery. These older guns lacked the firepower needed to destroy modern fortifications, but their large stocks of ammunition permitted sustained bombardment against lesser-fortified targets. Field commanders praised the performance of the 30.5cm Skoda mortar but viewed the 28cm coastal guns (which were not built as siege guns) and the 42cm Gamma and Skoda howitzers less favourably because of their limited mobility.

In sum, the siege guns' contribution to the German Army's campaigns in Poland, Belgium, France and the Soviet Union was negligible. The guns failed to rapidly or decisively destroy the fortifications they shelled and did not change the course of any battle in which they were used.

BIBLIOGRAPHY

Hogg, Ian V., *German Artillery of World War Two*, Greenhill Books (1997)

Jentz, Tomas L., *Big Bertha's Big Brother – Karl-Geraet (60cm) & (54cm)*, Panzer Tracts (2001)

Kleinert, Uwe, *Organisationsgeschichte der deutschen Heeresartillerie im II. Weltkrieg*, Herstellung und Verlag, BoD – Books on Demand (2017)

Prasil, Michal, *Skoda Heavy Guns*, Schiffer Publishing Ltd (1997)

Romanych, Marc & Rupp, Martin, *Maginot Line 1940: Battles on the French Frontier*, Osprey Publishing (2010)

Romanych, Marc & Rupp, Martin, *42cm 'Big Bertha' and German Siege Artillery of World War I*, Osprey Publishing (2013)

Rostislav, Aliev, *The Siege of Brest 1941: A Legend of Red Army Resistance on the Eastern Front*, Pen and Sword Books Ltd (2013)

Taube, Gerhard, *Deutsche Eisenbahn Geschütze*, Motorbuch Verlag (1990)

INDEX

Figures in **bold** refer to illustrations.
Plates are shown with page locaters in brackets.